LISTFUL LIVING

A List-Making Journey to a Less Stressed You

D0110700

Published by Mango Publishing Group, a division of Mango Media Inc.

Layout & Cover Design: Elina Diaz

For permission requests, please contact the publisher at:

Mango Publishing Group

2850 S Douglas Road, 2nd Floor

Coral Gables, FL 33134 USA

info@mango.bz

For special orders, quantity sales, course adoptions and corporate sales, please email the publisher at sales@mango.bz. For trade and wholesale sales, please contact Ingram Publisher Services at customer.service@ingramcontent.com or +1.800.509.4887.

Listful Living: A List-Making Journey to a Less Stressed You

Library of Congress Cataloging-in-Publication number: 2019944134
ISBN: (print) 978-1-64250-047-9, (ebook) 978-1-64250-048-6
BISAC category code: SELF-HELP / Self-Management / Time Management

Printed in the United States of America

LISTFUL LIVING

A List-Making Journey to a Less Stressed You

PAULA RIZZO

Author of the bestselling *Listful Thinking*

CORAL GABLES

For Jay Berman. You're my favorite.

TABLE OF CONTENTS

HOW TO USE THIS BOOK

My intention with this book is to guide you to become a calmer, more balanced, and less stressed version of yourself through list making.

This isn't journaling for journaling's sake.

The journalist in me wouldn't have it. We're going to walk through what needs to happen to make sure you have systems in place to be less stressed for good.

This book is designed to give you space and time to explore where you are, where you'd like to be, and how to get there in terms of your productivity and stress levels.

First, we'll evaluate where you are and what systems you're using while tapping into your personal productivity style. Then we'll dive into where you're going and how you want your life to truly look and feel. And because I'm a practical lady, I need to make sure that, by the time you finish this book, you'll have a roadmap to implement all of this.

There are three parts, and I'd love it if you trust the way I've organized it. It's meant to be filled out in order. I've been very intentional about structuring it so each part builds on the next.

That said, if sometimes you want to jump around and fill out a different page in the section you're working on, I won't tell anyone. Sometimes that can keep the momentum going. But for the most part—use this book in order.

Part One is your Personal GPS. I want you to lay out exactly where you are right now. This is the self-discovery phase. Put on your journalist hat, be as objective as possible, and note what is true right now. There are no judgments or ideas of what you think you should be doing. Just record what you're doing now.

Part Two is all about your Blue-Sky Intentions. If I were to take a peek into the future with you, what would I see? How would you feel? What would you be doing? I want you to imagine big in this phase. Don't worry about how you'll get there yet.

Part Three is your Passport to Stress-Free Living. This is the road-mapping stage where you'll explore how you'll get to the amazing place you envisioned in Part Two. This will have the tools and rules of engagement to ensure that you're living a less stressed and more productive life.

Don't get hung up on having the "right answers." There's no one way to do this and this is your personal journal—no one else's. Make it work for you!

People ask me all the time what pen I use or what journal I like, and I always say it doesn't actually matter. I say that in the kindest way possible because the truth is you need to find what works for you. And that's the right way to do it!

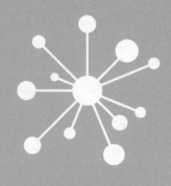

INSTRUCTIONS:
YOU WILL WRITE IN THIS BOOK!

If you're like me, you have a hard time writing in a book no matter how pretty it is. I grew up with a strict librarian who said, "Never write in these books; you must preserve them for others to enjoy."

Here's the thing though—this book is solely for you! No one else ever needs to see it.

The intent is to indulge. Indulge in writing on the pages of this book—IN PEN.

Yep, I said it. You can use pen! Gasp. I know. It's a big deal. Breathe. I'm going to do it too.

GETTING STARTED

WRITE WHAT COMES TO MIND FIRST

What did you eat for breakfast this morning?

What was your nickname when you were a kid?

Where was your favorite vacation ever?

What advice would you give your eight-year-old self?

CIRCLE YOUR FAVORITE

 Coffee or tea

 Salty or sweet

 Vanilla or chocolate

 Palm trees or spruce trees

 Plane or train

 Digital lists or paper lists

DOODLE ZONE

Draw a picture of a flower:

Make a few figure 8's:

Freestyle your favorite doodle here:

NICE WORK!

REST IS THE NEW HUSTLE

Turns out having an organ explode inside your body can be the nudge you need to slow down.

I know because it happened to me.

In January 2016, exactly one year after my first book, *Listful Thinking*, was published, I was sitting at my desk in Midtown Manhattan at Fox News, and I started to feel a dull pain below my belly button.

I was a senior health producer at the time, so I had spent nearly a decade interviewing doctors and nurses and knew my way in and out of hospitals, emergency rooms, and ORs.

But I'd never actually been in one as a patient.

I should have gone to see a doctor sooner. But I didn't.

I waited too long to get to the emergency room. Two days too long.

I wouldn't have guessed it, but I have a pretty high tolerance for pain. My appendix burst right inside my body.

Even when the doctors told me, I didn't believe them. I tried to convince them and myself that it was food poisoning. It was not.

A ruptured appendix is like a dirty bomb going off in your body, and it nearly cost me my life.

The toxins that my appendix had captured were set loose in my system. This caused all kinds of complications. I didn't realize how serious it was at the time, because, well, painkillers.

During my eight-day stay at New York Presbyterian–Weill Cornell on the Upper East Side of Manhattan, I didn't eat solid foods much at all. I lost twelve pounds and had bruises up and down my arms from IVs, blood draws, and injections.

I had three roommates during my stay, and one that I'm convinced I will be writing a novel about. Stay tuned for that.

My doctor took me out of work for six weeks. I thought he was crazy at first, but soon it started to sink in.

I was so weak when I left the hospital. I couldn't even lift my arms, pull myself up in bed, or basically move. I was hunched over like a little old lady and moved like a snail.

There were days when taking a shower was my only activity. That was it.

And the ordeal would consume my entire day. I would psych myself up to take the shower, actually do it, and then was so exhausted afterwards I would need to lie down.

I was too exhausted to even watch TV at times. My body was working overtime to heal itself.

People who know me, know I'm all about productivity and efficiency. They said to me, "You must be getting so much done on medical leave."

Nope.

The only thing I could do was rest. Literally, that was it.

This is difficult for anyone. But for me it was unthinkable. I never sat still before this.

I just published my first book the year before, and 2015 was a whirlwind for me.

If there was a networking event, I was at it.

"Want to meet for tea?" I'm in.

I was invited to book signings and speaking gigs and podcasts to promote my book, and I said yes to every single one. I wanted to get my book and my name out there. I was trying to figure out where to focus my time and energy, but that was really hard. So I just said yes to everything.

Plus, I was launching online products on my websites ListProducer.com and PaulaRizzo.com, and being an entrepreneur is all about the hustle and getting exposure. I had a commitment almost every day of the week.

That was on top of my full-time demanding job as a senior TV producer. Plus, all my obligations as a wife, daughter, and friend.

I like structure and planning for every single detail ahead of time. It's part of what has made me successful as a producer. I'm always one step ahead, anticipating where the plan will break down so I can have a backup ready to quickly fix things.

Except—you can't do that when your body breaks down. You have to let your doctors and nurses take over.

And there's nothing you can do but rest.

This experience reshaped how I view everything in my life. My family, my friends, my business, my book, my career, and all my commitments.

Now I work for myself as a media trainer, strategist, and speaker. Building a business is rewarding, challenging, and very stressful.

I have tools now that I've developed to ensure I don't get overwhelmed or burst more organs!

This has changed what I say yes to and what I say no to. I live my life with much more intention. I'm purposeful and mindful of every decision I make and where I spend my time.

Life is really what you make it, and you must make it work for you. The only way to do that is to set boundaries.

Rest really is the new hustle.

I offloaded a lot from my plate to recover. Basically everything. Every dinner, meeting, phone call, podcast, and speaking engagement came off my calendar because I truly needed to rest.

Slowing down is "prioritizing on steroids."

I always hated what Tim Ferriss says about how he decides which opportunities/interviews/events he will take on. He says if it's not a "Hell yeah"—it's a no.

But now I really get his point.

Except I'd prefer to go with the Marie Kondo (who I met just days before my appendix burst by the way) version of that: if it doesn't bring me joy, I'm not doing it anymore!

This experience has opened up something in me.

Maybe that little appendix was weighing me down in unknown ways. All I know is that I'm thrilled to guide you on your own list-making journey to be less stressed too.

MORE LIST-MAKING TIPS & TRICKS

I always wanted to write a book, but I never thought it would be about lists!

Before *Listful Thinking* and *Listful Living*, there was my blog at ListProducer.com. It's my love letter to all things list making. Check it out for tips and tricks to up your list-making game.

PART ONE

YOUR PERSONAL GPS—
WHERE ARE YOU?

Before we can dive into any of this work, you need to get a baseline and know where you're at right now, in this moment. What matters to you? What are you tolerating? What's working? What's not working? Etc.

Not last week or tomorrow—but right now. Where are you in the present?

As you work through this section of the book, I want you to be really focused on answering the questions and being honest about where you are right now. Then we'll build on this throughout this list-making journey.

GET IN TOUCH WITH THE "NOW" WITH MINDFULNESS

As a journalist, I've done many stories about meditation, mindfulness, and their many benefits. To be honest though, I was always a little iffy about it. Kind of like Dan Harris from ABC News, author of *10% Happier*; he's the ultimate skeptic. It must be a journalist thing. I've always struggled to switch my brain off or have an "enlightening moment" like everyone talks about.

Well, it turns out I was doing it wrong. My intentions were all screwed up.

But thanks to Oprah (of course) and Deepak Chopra, plus an all-day meditation retreat with world-renowned meditation teacher Sharon Salzberg, I figured it out.

If you know me personally or have read my other book, *Listful Thinking*, you know I have a generally positive and sunny outlook on the world. It's what many people tell me is one of my best qualities.

After my appendix burst in 2016—I envisioned 2017 being the "Great Restart."

Sadly, it wasn't.

I had an irritating gray cloud over my head.

I just couldn't shake the feelings of hopelessness and sadness. These are not emotions I usually keep around long, so it was particularly frustrating.

I told my mother, "I just need to do something to pull myself out of it." She suggested I do the 21-Day Meditation Challenge that was coming up in a few days with Oprah and Deepak Chopra.

I'd interviewed Deepak about meditation several times and liked him a lot, but I often found myself lost in his words and not totally grasping what I should be doing.

But I said, "Sure, I'll try it."

At the same time, a meditation company for busy professionals called The Path in New York City was running an all-day meditation retreat with author and teacher Sharon Salzberg.

I was able to ask Sharon a question during the retreat, "People who meditate a lot often say when they're having a problem or challenge that they 'meditate' on it and the answer comes to them. That never happens to me. What am I doing wrong?"

She said, "Nothing. It doesn't work like that."

And just like that I was freed from the idea that I had to get an immediate result from meditation. It was my *Ohhh, now I get it* moment.

It's not as simple as just doing this thing and suddenly having all the answers to my dilemmas. Got it.

Once I made that very big realization, a huge weight was lifted.

Now, I meditate for ten minutes on most days using an app called Calm. I have to say the cumulative benefit is that I feel happier, am more focused, and can slow down before reacting to things immediately. It allows me to pause and take things in more easily.

Benefits of Mindfulness

- Better focus

- Increased productivity

- Reduced anxiety

- Boosted attention span

- Enhanced self-awareness

"To really do nothing, with perfection, is as difficult as doing everything."

—Alan Watts

Essentialism for You

I'm an essentialist. But I wasn't always that way, and it's hard to maintain. It takes work. Simply put—essentialism is the pursuit of less.

If you haven't read *Essentialism* by Greg McKeown, you must!

Once you strip everything back to just the few things that matter most, your days become so much more manageable. I highly recommend this way of thinking for anyone who says, "I'm so busy" like it's your personal mantra.

Prioritize Your Life

#1: What are your top priorities in life?

Think really high level here—what matters to you most overall?

I listed a few to get you started, but fill in the blanks and circle the ones that resonate most with you.

Sleep   Money   Nutrition   Travel   Work   Meditation   Family

_____   _____   _____

_____   _____   _____

#2: Put these priorities in value order below. 1 is the most important and 10 is the least important.

1.
2.
3.
4.
5.
6.
7.
8.
9.
10.

#3: What is your #1 top priority?

Remember this priority might change over time, but I want to know what your top priority is right now. Don't feel like you have to get the "right" answer—write down what is most true for you. Don't write what you think you should write or what you wish was your priority.

Write your true #1 priority right now.

#4: Spread the word!

One of the best ways to remain accountable is to say something out loud. Share your true #1 priority with me and other *Listful Living* readers on social media!

- Tag me @ListProducer

- Use the hashtag #ListfulLiving so we can find each other!

Focus Spotlight

Pick your top five priorities from the list on page 32 and list them here:

1.

2.

3.

4.

5.

Use this pie chart to illustrate how much time you're currently giving these five priorities. Remember, your top priority might not be getting the most time and that's alright. This exercise is intended to figure out where you're spending your time. That's it—don't judge it.

Yes vs. No

What activities and commitments did you say YES to this year?

HOME/FAMILY

_____
_____
_____
_____
_____

WORK

_____
_____
_____
_____
_____

COMMUNITY

_____
_____
_____
_____
_____

SELF-CARE

_____

_____

_____

_____

_____

HEALTH

_____

_____

_____

_____

_____

PERSONAL DEVELOPMENT

_____

_____

_____

_____

_____

_____

_____

SOCIAL LIFE

_____

_____

_____

_____

_____

What activities and commitments did you say NO to this year?

HOME/FAMILY

_____

_____

_____

_____

_____

WORK

_____

_____

_____

_____

_____

COMMUNITY

_____

_____

_____

_____

_____

SELF-CARE

_____

_____

_____

_____

_____

HEALTH

_____

_____

_____

_____

_____

_____

_____

PERSONAL DEVELOPMENT

_____

_____

_____

_____

_____

SOCIAL LIFE

_____

_____

_____

_____

_____

YOUR PRODUCTIVITY STYLE

One of the biggest hurdles people face when they're trying to be more organized is figuring out what style works for them. It's why I recommend a variety of apps and tips on my site ListProducer.com. If you're not a morning person, I don't want you to become one: it will make you cranky and resentful. Trust me, I've tried.

There is no one solution that suits everyone. Once you understand your productivity style, you can cater your work schedule around your needs to be less stressed.

Word Play for Productivity

Set a timer for five minutes and write down any words or
phrases that come to your mind regarding your productivity
today. Do not edit this list—just write as you feel the thoughts
bubble up.

_____

_____

_____

_____

_____

_____

_____

_____

_____

_____

_____

_____

_____

But, Why?

Now set a timer for fifteen minutes and free write about why you feel this way.

Be very specific here.

What is working or not working when it comes to your productivity and stress levels?

Write it out here. If you would prefer to type, go for it but then do a bit of an arts and crafts project and print out your thoughts and paste them to this page.

_____

_____

_____

_____

_____

_____

_____

_____

_____

Look, Listen, and Learn

Knowing the environment that will optimize your productivity and make you feel less stressed will help you cross tasks from your to-do list with ease.

I've spent my career working in busy and loud newsrooms with lots of people talking and scurrying around me. I got used to tuning everyone out to get my work done. So, when I started writing my first book, *Listful Thinking*, I struggled. I was writing alone at home, and it was too quiet.

I realized that to get any work done I had to turn the television on as background noise. And sometimes I need to get out of my house and go to a loud coffee shop to get started on a project. But once I realized that about myself, I became much more productive when I allowed myself to work the way that was most efficient for me.

Let's use your senses to determine the optimal environment for you.

Really try to put yourself into each of these situations, and be honest about how they make you feel. There's no right or wrong answer.

See

Do you find yourself getting distracted when you're in an open space with lots of people working around you? (Ex. coffee shop or office with an open floor plan)

What kind of lighting do you need when you're working on something important?

What do you like to look at when you're working?
(circle all that apply)

City	Waterfall
Skyline	Trees
Beach	Television
Artwork	Snow falling

Rank these spots (and any you fill in on your own) in the order you'd like to spend the day working there.

Circle one that is the "best spot ever!"

Beach   Café/Restaurant

Quiet Office   Outdoors/Park

Home Office   Library

Bustling Office   Hotel

What colors are prominent in your work space?

Do you have a lot of artwork around you?

Are there plants in your work environment?

What kind of objects are on your desk?

Hear

How do you feel when you're working in a quiet place?

How much work are you able to do in a busy or loud environment?

Can you do work with the television on?

The Power of Music

Music has been proven to help get your productivity juices flowing. Just fifteen minutes of the music of your choice can put you back on track. However, listening to favorite songs while working could set some people back because they just want to sing the whole time. Try both methods and see what works better for you.

What kind of music, if any, do you like to listen to when you're working?

What do you feel when you listen to that kind of music?

What song gets you pumped up to get things done?

How long do you need to listen to that music to get in the mood to work? (Try it now!)

Smell

Do you use essential oils?

Which ones? How does it make you feel?

Do you drink coffee or tea when you're working?

How does that help you focus?

Do you have flowers in your work space?

Do you light candles when you work?

If yes, what scents do you like best?

Touch

Describe what your desk feels like.

Describe what the chair you sit on feels like.

What kind of pen or pencil do you like to use when you write?

Do you use a mouse or a touchpad when you use a computer?

Describe the list or journal paper you like to use.

The Golden Hour of Productivity

In photography, "the golden hour" is the most optimal time for any type of photo, because the light is perfectly diffused and warm. It happens right after sunrise or before sunset.

Answer these questions to determine your own personal "golden hour of productivity":

How productive do you feel in the morning?

What time do you start to feel sluggish during the day?

How much can you get done before lunch?

What kind of work do you like to do before lunch? (Phone calls, cleaning, writing, etc.)

How productive do you feel after lunch?

When you have to get work done in the afternoon, how productive are you? Check all that apply:

- ☐ I can plow through my to-do list in a flash
- ☐ I'm mostly looking at the clock and not getting much done
- ☐ I can't get anything done in the afternoon
- ☐ There are certain tasks I'm better at in the afternoon like _____

If you're doing work in the evening, how do you feel? Circle all that apply:

Productive Happy Resentful

Sluggish Angry Grateful

Fired up Stressed Motivated

Looking back at your answers—what is your most productive time of day?

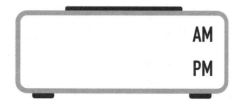

Creativity Tip: Wait 'Til You're Sleepy

Sounds crazy but it's true.

Turns out, when you're sleepy, the rational mind is tired and the imaginative mind starts to take over. That means your inner critic is taking a bit of a break to allow your ideas to flow.

I have the pleasure of knowing and studying with Suzanne Kingsbury, who is an author and leading expert on creativity. She's the founder of Gateless Writing, Inc., an organization that moves writers to the point of publication using ancient Zen practices and neuroscience.

"The same brain waves (theta) fire when you are sleepy as when you are dreaming and in deep meditation. In this state, brainstorming can be easy; new approaches come flooding in, and your creativity becomes spatial rather than linear," Kingsbury said.

In 2011, psychologist Marieke Wieth at Albion University in Michigan did a study of 428 students to test their ability to do menial tasks when they were tired.

The students identified as night owls, early birds, or neutral and were given tasks to do during their optimal alert and non-alert times.

The results, recorded in the journal *Thinking & Reasoning*, were that they performed just as well regardless of the time when it came to analytical problems.

But when given a creative task? Yep—you guessed it…sleepy time equals productive time.

"It is often tempting to use exhaustion as an excuse to not work on a project. In fact, if you can allow your mind to wander onto a project or a challenge when you are tired, you can move through stuckness and find a surprising landscape of new ideas," Kingsbury said.

Schedule your creative tasks accordingly!

Best Day Ever!

Studies have shown that Tuesdays are actually the most productive day of the week. But of course that's not true for everyone. We'll get to the bottom of your ideal workday. Weekends count too.

Task#1: List out the types of tasks you do in a given week.

Take this week for example—write out everything you did, including write articles, talk to clients on the phone, write emails, care for an elderly parent, care for a child, make dinner, go to yoga, meditate, etc.

WORK TASKS   HOME TASKS

_____   _____

_____   _____

_____   _____

_____   _____

_____   _____

_____   _____

_____   _____

_____   _____

_____   _____

_____   _____

_____   _____

_____   _____

Task #2: Which days do you currently do each of the tasks above? Write next to each task the days you typically do it. If you do all tasks on all days, that's ok too. Note it above using these abbreviations:

Monday—M
Tuesday—Tu
Wednesday—W
Thursday—Th
Friday—F
Saturday—Sa
Sunday—Su
All days—All

Task #3: Note which tasks are easy to do and which are more difficult by putting an E or a D next to each one.

Task #4: Looking back at last week, which was your most efficient day?

Canceled Meetings?

What do you do when someone cancels an appointment with you? (Circle one or add to the list)

Start working on the next to-do list item

Call a friend/family member

Get a massage

Take a nap

Meditate

_____

_____

_____

_____

_____

_____

_____

_____

_____

_____

_____

What's Your Pomodoro?

The Pomodoro Technique was invented by Francesco Cirillo in the late 1980s. You set a timer, work for twenty-five minutes of focused time, and then take a break. It's called Pomodoro, which means "tomato" in Italian, because he used a little tomato timer when he was developing the method.

For me, I think twenty-five minutes is a bit too long at first. I can focus for about fifteen to twenty minutes at a time when I get into a groove. The trick is to try out a bunch of time intervals and see what works for you.

Task #1: Pick one task that you've been avoiding on your to-do list and write it here:

Task # 2: Set a timer for twenty-five minutes. If you get distracted, you must stop the clock. Try your hardest to focus on only that one task for the time allotted.

Take note of when your mind wanders and write it down here.

Task #3: Use this space to record how you feel about this exercise.

Here are some questions to guide you: Did that time feel long, short, or just right? How much of the task did you actually get done? Did that surprise you? When did you get distracted? What would help you stay on track with that task?

_____

_____

_____

_____

_____

_____

_____

_____

_____

_____

_____

Task #4: Now pick another item on your to-do list and write it here:

Task #5: Set a timer for fifteen minutes. (Stop the clock if you get distracted again.)

Task #6: Now use this space to record how you felt this time. What was different?

_____

_____

_____

_____

_____

_____

_____

_____

_____

_____

_____

_____

_____

_____

_____

_____

Task #7: Continue to do this until you find a time frame that makes you feel like you are getting something done, but not rushing. You may find that there are different time frames for different tasks.

Task # 8: Record how often you got distracted here.

Task # 9: Record your ideal Pomodoro here.

Time Tracking Challenge

There's probably a big difference between how long a task will actually take you and how long you *think* it will take you.

How many times have you said, "Oh this will just take five minutes," and then it ended up taking forty?

It happens to the best of us. But there's a way to find out exactly how long tasks will take you. Time yourself!

Pick Three

Pick three tasks that you often do throughout the week and list them here. These can be things you do at work or at home. Anything from regular meetings, putting on makeup, eating lunch, commuting to work, writing, phone calls, etc.

1.

2.

3.

How Long Does It Take?

As a TV producer, I'm uniquely aware of just what thirty seconds or a minute feel like. That's because in the news business you need to know how long each segment will take and every second counts. If a story runs long by fifteen seconds, then another story needs to be cut by the same amount of time so the newscast ends on time.

Much like news stories, this is what you should be doing with your daily tasks. I realize most people don't have that strange skill ingrained in their minds. So let's build that muscle.

The value is that you'll be able to easily swap out one task for another in your day if you know how long it will take you. Then you'll be able to fit tasks together like puzzle pieces to accomplish more in less time.

First, you need to figure out how long each task takes—and I mean actually takes…not how long you *think* it takes! Big difference.

Ready, Set, Time Yourself!

Take each task from above and time yourself the next time you do it.

Write down the time you "think" it will take in the "estimated time" slot and then how long it actually took in the "actual time" slot.

You might be surprised!

Task #1_____

Estimated time:

Actual time:

Task #2 _____

Estimated time:

Actual time:

Task #3 _____

Estimated time:

Actual time:

Now that you've done this challenge, what surprised you about it? Use this space to write your thoughts.

Tools for Tracking

Here are some tools for tracking your time:

Stopwatch: Use the stopwatch on your phone or watch the clock, but be honest. This only works if you're truthful. It's very important that the record keeping you do is accurate so you can better fit tasks into your day.

Toggl: A website that lets you track how long your tasks take. So those reports that will "only take a minute" can actually be tracked in real time. This is also a good way for your freelancers or vendors to log their time. That way, they know how long it takes to finish projects, and you can see how much you owe them if you pay by the hour. Toggl.com

Rescue Time: A web-based service similar to Toggl that will track the time you spend on your computer. It also allows you to set limits on how long you check emails or update social media. This helps keep you from getting distracted while you're supposed to be logging your time. RescueTime.com

Burnout Syndrome Is Real

It's official.

The World Health Organization now recognizes work "burnout syndrome" as an official medical diagnosis.

The WHO's International Classification of Diseases (ICD) says that burnout "result[s] from chronic workplace stress that has not been successfully managed."

Characteristics include:

- Feelings of energy depletion or exhaustion

- Increased mental distance from one's job or feelings of negativism or cynicism related to one's job

- Reduced professional efficacy

The Numbers (According to Stress.org)

- Up to 90 percent of all medical visits are stress related

- Chronic stress costs the US approximately six hundred billion dollars annually

"Stress is what happens in the gap between demand and capacity," says Heidi Hanna, PhD and author of *Stressaholic: 5 Steps to Transform Your Relationship with Stress.*

Stress Isn't All Bad

Hanna says stress is here to help us. The stress you feel about giving a presentation at work or doing something challenging actually will improve your body and mind.

"Your heart rate goes up to boost available energy as your memory is improved. You're laser focused and have a better attention span and extra energy. Plus, your immune function goes up temporarily to protect you," Hanna said.

However, stress becomes a problem when you don't give your body a chance to recover from the challenging situation.

"Did you really 'rest and digest' after giving a presentation? If not, that's where stress becomes chronic and unmanaged," she said.

Examine Your Stress Style

Pick a Scene

Pick one scene from the last two months where you felt your stress levels were through the roof.

Be as descriptive as possible—use your five senses to return to that time here. Give yourself ten minutes to write freely:

How Did It Feel?

List out how you felt specifically after that very stressful moment in your recent memory. Use single words or phrases to describe your feelings from the scene on the last page:

_____

_____

_____

_____

_____

_____

_____

_____

_____

_____

_____

_____

_____

_____

_____

_____

_____

_____

What Made It So Stressful?

Knowing your personality and capacity to get things done—
what made this situation especially stressful for you? Jot down a
few words or phrases that come to mind first:

_____

_____

_____

_____

_____

_____

_____

_____

_____

_____

_____

_____

_____

_____

_____

_____

Long-Term Effects

List out how this stressful situation affected your life at all these touch points in time.

How did it stick with you…

An hour later?

_____

_____

_____

_____

_____

_____

A day later?

_____

_____

_____

_____

_____

_____

A week later?

_____

_____

_____

_____

_____

_____

A month later?

_____

_____

_____

_____

_____

_____

How Do You Manifest Stress?

After years as a health journalist, I've done dozens and dozens of stories about the effect stress has on the body, mind, and soul.

It's important to identify how stress shows itself in your life so you can become aware of what's happening. You identified one scene above, but now I want you to think of other times you've been stressed and use those collective times to do this exercise.

Circle which symptoms you experience when you're stressed out and fill in any others that come to mind:

Stress on the Body

Headaches
Muscle pain
Back pain
Chest pain
Sleep problems
Upset stomach
Fatigue

_____

_____

_____

Stress on the Mind

Anxiety
Depression
Sadness
Lack of focus
Lack of motivation
Feeling overwhelmed
Anger

_____

_____

_____

STRESS ON YOUR HABITS	STRESS ON YOUR PERFORMANCE
Overeating	Missing appointments
Undereating	Missing deadlines
Biting nails	Becoming less dependable
Drug or alcohol use	Feeling scattered
Skipping exerciset	Feeling frozen
	Procrastinating

_____   _____

_____   _____

_____   _____

_____   _____

_____   _____

Other Stressful Situations

List out briefly three other times you've felt very stressed over
the past year.

1.

2.

3.

Common Theme Search

Now that you've examined this stressful slice of your life, what can you glean from that information? What is a recurring theme, if any, in the stressful moments of your life?

Perhaps a particular situation sets you up for stress? Maybe it was lack of sleep, not enough resources, or no time to prepare, etc. Write out what commonalities you see in these situations.

WHO—Are there certain people who are present during your stress scenes?

_____

_____

_____

_____

_____

WHAT—What are you doing during these stress scenes?

_____

_____

_____

_____

_____

WHERE—What is your location?

_____

_____

_____

_____

_____

WHEN—Is there a time of day or year that these stress scenes pop up?

_____

_____

_____

_____

_____

WHY—What are the circumstances of these stress scenes?

_____

_____

_____

_____

_____

What are the common denominators in these stress scenes? (Pull this from the information you've discovered above)

_____

_____

_____

_____

_____

Pick a Zen Scene

Think about a very peaceful time in your life in the past two months.

Pick just one scene from your life, and write about it here.

Use all five senses to be as descriptive as you can. Set a timer for ten minutes to write as much as you can.

_____

_____

_____

_____

_____

_____

How Did It Feel?

List out how you felt specifically after that very Zen moment in your recent memory. Use single words or phrases to describe your feelings from the scene above:

_____

_____

_____

_____

_____

What Made It So Peaceful?

Knowing your personality and capacity to get things done, what made this situation especially peaceful for you? Jot down a few words or phrases that come to mind first:

_____

_____

_____

_____

_____

_____

Long-Term Zen Effects

List out how this Zen situation affected your life at all these touch points in time. How did it stick with you...

An hour later?

_____

_____

_____

_____

A day later?

_____

_____

_____

_____

A week later?

_____

_____

_____

_____

A month later?

_____

_____

_____

_____

Your Destress Style

Self-care is a buzzword these days. I like to think of it as kind things you do for yourself. The benefits are immense because it will lead to an improved mood, boost productivity, and send your optimism soaring. It doesn't have to be a weeklong vacation in Mexico but rather small, deliberate actions you take that feed your mind, body, and soul.

What are your *current* self-care activities?

List them here, along with how often you actually do them and how they make you feel.

Self-Care Activity:	Frequency:	Feelings:
_____	_____	_____
_____	_____	_____
_____	_____	_____
_____	_____	_____
_____	_____	_____

Share Your Favorite Self-Care Activity

Take your favorite self-care activity from the list above and share it with me on social media. Tag me @ListProducer and use the hashtag #ListfulLiving.

PART TWO

YOUR BLUE-SKY INTENTIONS— WHERE ARE YOU GOING?

Get ready to get dreamy!

Part One was all about how your life is right now. In this section, I want you to drift off into the future. This is all about where you're going.

Don't worry about *how* you'll get there. Instead, focus on how you'd like your life to feel and look.

I always got a kick out of Conan O'Brien's skit, "In the Year 2000," about what life would be like in the future. I watched his show almost every night when I worked as a copy editor and producer at WPIX in New York City after I returned home from my own ten o'clock broadcast. The best part of the skit was that he kept doing it well into the 2000s, which made it even funnier.

He'd map out how the world would look when all medical procedures took less than thirty minutes, robots did all our housework, and scientists discovered the secret ingredient in Starbucks coffee. Spoiler alert: It's a chemical that makes you forget that you're paying four bucks for a cup of coffee!

I want you to let your creativity roam in this section. Remember, this is all about what is possible—not how you'll get there (yet).

"You become what you believe."

—Oprah Winfrey

Design Your Ideal...

Good Morning!

Let's start the day off right every single morning.

Use this space to write about how you'd like to feel when you wake up in the morning. Remember this is all about how you *want* to feel—not what you feel right now. We're in a dream state.

How does your head feel?

_____

_____

_____

_____

How does your body feel?

_____

_____

_____

_____

_____

_____

What is around you?

_____

_____

_____

_____

List out words here to describe how you start your day:

_____   _____   _____

_____   _____   _____

_____   _____   _____

_____   _____   _____

What foods do you eat in the morning?

_____

_____

_____

_____

What other activities do you do in the morning?

_____

_____

_____

_____

What is the first thing you do in the morning?

_____

_____

_____

_____

What do you do after that?

_____

_____

_____

_____

Good Evening!

What would you like your evenings to look like in the future?
Think about that sweet wind down time as the sun sets—what
do you want for yourself?

Where do you spend your evenings?

_____

_____

_____

_____

What do you like to be doing at night?

_____

_____

_____

_____

Who is with you?

_____

_____

_____

_____

What do your surroundings look like?

_____

_____

_____

_____

When your head hits the pillow, what do you want to feel?

_____

_____

_____

_____

Write out all the words that describe that moment here:

_____   _____   _____

_____   _____   _____

_____   _____   _____

_____   _____   _____

Set Up Your Weeks

In the space below, chart out your dream scenarios.

This can be a work schedule or a home itinerary—whatever you'd like. Fill in when you'll do work, when you'll play, when you'll take breaks, etc.

DAY
Morning
Afternoon
Evening

Monday

Tuesday

Wednesday

Thursday

Friday

Saturday

Sunday

Saturday

Sunday

1

2

3

4

5

6

7

8

9

10

11

12

13

14

15

16

17

18

19

20

21

22

23

24

25

26

27

28

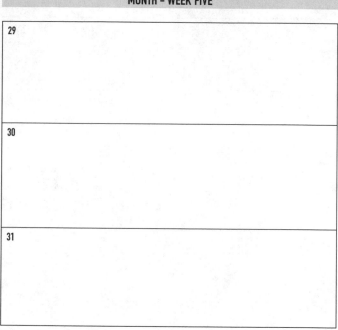

29

30

31

GREAT WORK!

Choose Your Friends Wisely

It's important to notice how you feel when you are around certain people, rather than how you think you should feel. Here's how Suzanne Kingsbury, creativity expert and founder of Gateless Writing, Inc., explained it to me.

"If you're around someone and find yourself feeling shut down, constricted, or low in self-esteem, the amygdala in the brain has been triggered. Some kind of threat has been detected, and you are in a very mild state of fight or flight. From there, it's almost impossible to access the imaginative mind and the intuit.

"When you are around someone who makes you feel good, who supports and buoys the best parts of you, the prefrontal cortex opens, serotonin and other 'happy' neurotransmitters fire, and, in this 'feel good' state, you can often be at your most productive," she said.

Priority People

List who makes you feel the most calm and balanced in your life here:

AT WORK:	AT HOME:	IN YOUR COMMUNITY:
_____	_____	_____
_____	_____	_____
_____	_____	_____
_____	_____	_____

Who makes you feel the most stressed out?

AT WORK:	AT HOME:	IN YOUR COMMUNITY:
_____	_____	_____
_____	_____	_____
_____	_____	_____
_____	_____	_____

Sprinkle Your Days with Your Favorite People

If you had a perfect scenario, who would you see more of and how often?

_____

_____

_____

_____

_____

_____

_____

_____

_____

_____

_____

_____

You can include people from your *personal life* here:

EVERYDAY:	TWICE A WEEK:	EVERY WEEK:
_____	_____	_____
_____	_____	_____
_____	_____	_____
_____	_____	_____

EVERY MONTH:	EVERY QUARTER:	TWICE A YEAR:
_____	_____	_____
_____	_____	_____
_____	_____	_____
_____	_____	_____

EVERY YEAR:

_____

_____

_____

_____

Get Down to Business

Who are some of the people you'd like to check in with to grow your business or career? How often?

EVERYDAY:

_____

_____

_____

_____

TWICE A WEEK:

_____

_____

_____

_____

EVERY WEEK:

_____

_____

_____

_____

EVERY MONTH:

_____

_____

_____

_____

EVERY QUARTER:

_____

_____

_____

_____

TWICE A YEAR:

_____

_____

_____

_____

EVERY YEAR:

_____

_____

_____

_____

The Perfect Workspace

Think about what inspires you to work. Where are you sitting? What are you looking at? Who is around you?

Free write or draw here what the perfect workspace will look like for you:

A Matter of Health

Staying healthy should be at the top of your list, but it takes work.

In a perfect world, what activities or appointments will keep you healthy? How often would you do them and check in on your health matters? We're talking about both physical and mental health here.

EVERYDAY:

_____
_____
_____

TWICE A WEEK:

_____
_____
_____

EVERY WEEK:

_____
_____
_____

EVERY MONTH:

_____
_____
_____

EVERY QUARTER:

_____
_____

TWICE A YEAR:

_____
_____

EVERY YEAR:

_____
_____
_____

Determine Where Your Time Is Best Spent

Yes List!

This might be the most important list you write in this book.

It's the list of the things you want to make time for most in your life. Don't worry about when you'll do these things, but just that you want to do them.

This can also be thought of like a Bucket List or Dream List.

Professionally:

_____

_____

_____

_____

At home:

_____

_____

_____

_____

In your community:

_____

_____

_____

_____

Socially:

_____

_____

_____

_____

Financially:

_____

_____

_____

_____

Travel:

_____

_____

_____

_____

Personal Development:

_____

_____

_____

_____

Events to attend:

_____

_____

_____

_____

Books to read:

_____

_____

_____

_____

Movies/TV shows to see:

_____

_____

_____

_____

People to meet:

_____

_____

_____

_____

Restaurants to try:

_____

_____

_____

_____

Use this blank space to write out any other things you'd like to add to your "Yes List":

Subtraction Project

Sometimes, what you subtract from your life is just as important as what you add.

My friend and colleague Cass McCrory created the Subtraction Project to help overwhelmed people subtract the extra in their home, inbox, and brain so life adds up to what you truly want.

In her own experience, she found her life wasn't "adding up" so she went to Target and added stuff to her cart.

But that didn't do it for her. She needed to subtract. And, as she did, she felt more balance in her life. She started to share her "stuff" subtractions.

She hosts email challenges which prompt you to delete the stuff around you, in your inbox or brain, that is weighing you down.

Check it out at SubtractionProject.com.

The "No Thank You" List!

These are the things that Marie Kondo would say "do not spark joy!"

These are the activities that you'd like to cut out of your life altogether or do less of.

Perhaps these are things that used to bring you joy but do not anymore.

Be honest here.

Professionally:

_____

_____

_____

_____

At home:

_____

_____

_____

_____

In your community:

_____

_____

_____

_____

_____

_____

Socially:

_____

_____

_____

_____

Financially:

_____

_____

_____

_____

Travel:

_____

_____

_____

_____

Personal Development:

_____

_____

_____

_____

_____

_____

_____

_____

_____

_____

_____

Use this blank space to write out any other things you'd like to add to your "No Thank You" list:

Checklist of Fun

List out the things you absolutely love doing that get you charged up!

It could be running, reading, cooking, watching movies, visiting new places, etc.

Task #1: List them all out here.

_____

_____

_____

_____

_____

_____

_____

_____

_____

Task #2: Now go back and make a note next to each one of
how often you'd like to do these in the future.

"E" for everyday

"W" for weekly

"BW" for bi-weekly

"M" for monthly

"BM" for bi-monthly

"A" for annually

"SA" for semi-annually

"When you say yes to others, make sure you are not saying no to yourself."

—Paulo Coelho

RENEW WITH SELF-CARE

When was the last time you gave yourself a gift?

Sure, it could have been a diamond ring or a sports car—but it doesn't have to be.

The idea behind self-care is kindness that you aim toward yourself. This can be taking a nap, talking to your best friend, or getting your nails done. It doesn't have to be a big, grand gesture—sometimes the simpler, the better.

Give yourself time to recharge with things you enjoy doing, so you can improve your well-being. Research shows that practicing self-care can make you feel less stressed and more empowered.

A Vacation Could Save Your Life!

A forty-year Finnish study published in the *Journal of Nutrition, Health & Aging* found taking vacations could prolong life.

The study followed 1,222 middle-aged male executives who had some risk of cardiovascular disease.

One group was given advice to eat well, get more sleep, take medicine, etc. The other group wasn't given any advice.

Turns out the group without any advice actually lived longer than the other group. This made researchers scratch their heads and dig a bit deeper.

Vacations seemed to be the tipping point here. They asked who took three weeks of vacation.

Here's what they found—the men who took shorter vacations worked more and slept less than those who took longer vacations.

So any cardiovascular benefits that the men who were given advice had achieved were erased when they slacked on their vacation time.

Vacations are a great way to relieve stress.

To be clear, this isn't a selfish act. Self-care is an act of nurturing your body, mind, or soul.

I try to incorporate self-help activities into my life whenever possible.

For example, I always give myself an extra day off when I return from a trip. This allows me to return less stressed, and I'm able to reset before jumping back into work mode. This has become non-negotiable for me.

I also make sure to carve out time in my calendar to eat lunch every day. I know it might sound silly, but it's really important to me that I eat so I'm not cranky. I structure my media-training coaching calls and other appointments around it.

What about you?

Circle which of these things would feel good to you (or modify them to work):

An extra five minutes in bed in the morning

Time to watch your favorite TV show

Buying a new notebook

Drinking a cup of your favorite tea

Having a glass of wine with a friend

Getting a massage

Going on a vacation

Giving yourself fifteen minutes to research your next vacation

Playing with a puppy or kitten

Painting or drawing

Meditating for ten minutes

Going to a yoga class

Calling a friend

Going for a walk

Writing a gratitude list

Turning off social media for the afternoon

Shutting off your cell phone after eight o'clock in the evening

Taking a nap

Writing in a journal

Giving yourself an extra day off after returning from vacation

Setting aside time for lunch every day

List out some of the other things that would give your soul a break and allow you to be reinvigorated:

hygge, n.—(pronounced: "hoo-gah") A quality of coziness and comfortable conviviality that engenders a feeling of contentment or well-being (regarded as a defining characteristic of Danish culture)

Example: "Why not follow the Danish example and bring more hygge into your daily life?"

Source: Oxford English Dictionary

Let's Hear It for the Hygge

I like to think of hygge as a hug.

That's pretty close to what it actually is. It roughly translates to "cozy" from Danish.

I first learned about the concept of hygge from my media-training client Melissa Coleman. Melissa is the author of *The Minimalist Kitchen: The Practical Art of Making More with Less*, and she regularly practices hygge.

She says it's all about finding things that make you happy and incorporating them into your everyday life.

Think: loungewear, blankets, tea, a good book—these are all excellent ways to practice hygge.

In her book, Melissa says, "Self-care doesn't have to be extravagant or costly."

I couldn't agree more!

Check out my interview with Melissa Coleman here for more on how to turn your kitchen into the most organized space in your house: bit.ly/PaulaMelissaVideo.

Hobbies & Hygge for Your To-Do List

Having hobbies you love to do can enhance your self-care routine.

For me, I love to read novels before bed, and I'm obsessed with watching *Golden Girls* reruns. These are hobbies of mine that make me feel energized and happy.

I believe in being a lifelong learner and am always adding to my hobbies list. Currently, I'm working on learning Italian using the Babbel app. *Ciao!*

What are some hobbies or skills you've always wanted to learn and would make you feel invigorated?

List them here. Remember, don't worry about how you're going to do these:

Ikigai

My friend Terri Trespicio gave me a book called *Ikigai: The Japanese Secret to a Long and Happy Life* because she knew it would be right up my alley. And it is!

Ikigai is a Japanese word that translates roughly into "the happiness of always being busy."

I've also seen it translated as "a reason for being" or "what you get up for in the morning."

The concept of ikigai is a bit different from hygge. Hygge is about slowing down and giving yourself a break whereas ikigai is about giving yourself a purpose.

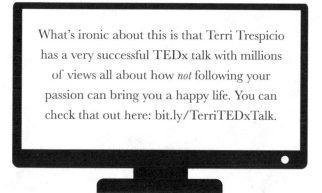

What's ironic about this is that Terri Trespicio has a very successful TEDx talk with millions of views all about how *not* following your passion can bring you a happy life. You can check that out here: bit.ly/TerriTEDxTalk.

The book's authors, Hector Garcia and Francesc Miralles, go on a mission to study the secrets of Japanese centenarians. They visit Okinawa because its residents have the highest life expectancy in the world.

What they found there were residents who smiled, laughed, and generally loved life. They lived well into their hundreds and had fewer chronic illnesses than other people in their age range.

So what gives?

Examples of Ikigai:

1. Growing your own vegetables

2. Being a good friend

3. Standing up for something you believe in

4. Drawing

5. Writing

6. Helping the elderly

7. Adopting a pet

8. Hosting dinner parties

9. Making animals out of butter (No really, I know someone's great aunt who did this. It's a skill.)

Here's the thing—ikigai doesn't need to be complicated or too over the top. It's about choosing an activity that will keep you busy but blissful.

What's Your Ikigai?

Share Your Ikigai with Me!

Take a photo of you doing that activity and share it on social media. Tag me @ListProducer and use #ListfulLiving

"Gratitude is one of the sweet shortcuts to finding peace of mind and happiness inside."

—Barry Neil Kaufman

Gratitude List

Off the top of your head, list three things that you're grateful for today.

They don't have to be grand things like getting a promotion or buying a new apartment.

Instead, focus on the things that might *seem ordinary*—like mangos being in season or that you got to talk to your college friend today.

Don't overthink it—go!

1.

2.

3.

Taking time out of your day to write down what you're grateful for will retrain your brain. Evolution has actually conditioned us to be highly biased toward negative information. That's because it could be a threat to our well-being.

"Since focusing on negative information is our natural state, we need to make actual effort to focus on the positive," Dr.

Ben Michaelis, a psychologist and elite-performance coach based in New York City, told me.

He also said the more you can get into the habit of focusing on things that you are grateful for, the better you feel. There's lots of research-based evidence to back this up.

"For example, one study found that people who keep gratitude journals for eight weeks are happier, more satisfied with their lives, and have lower stress and less inflammation than control groups," he said.

"Life moves pretty fast.
If you don't stop and look
around once in a while,
you could miss it."

—*Ferris Bueller's
Day Off*

Gratitude Habit Challenge

Have you ever started to feel sorry for yourself and gotten into a real funk?

The gratitude list can help. Other experts will tell you to do one every single day. And yes, that is beneficial. But I want you to find this helpful and not see it as a chore.

So here's my challenge to you—can you take a *pause* when you realize that something has just happened that made you grateful in the moment?

Awareness is the name of the game here.

So being able to recognize something that you're grateful for in the moment and savoring it will condition your brain to look for those moments.

Then write it down. Somewhere, anywhere.

It can be in Evernote, or in a notebook, or even in an email to yourself. Or share it on social media and tag me @ListProducer and use the hashtag #ListfulLiving.

The important thing is to build this gratitude habit.

I'm a big fan of *The Office*, and there's a line that Ed Helm's character, Andy Bernard, says that always sticks in my head.

Toward the end of the series, he says, "I wish there was a way to know you're in the good old days before you've actually left them."

Oh wow. So so true, right?

Think back to some of your best memories—don't you wish you savored them a little more?

Without getting too woo-woo—this is a practice in mindful meditation.

Being aware of the present and how you feel in it will allow you to really enjoy and remember the moment. Plus, it will help you to truly realize that you have a lot to be grateful for.

Where will you record your gratitude for this challenge?

SET AN INTENTION FOR YOUR FUTURE

I'll never forget that one of my favorite teachers made us write letters to our future selves in grade school.

For the assignment, we had to tell ourselves what we thought our lives in the future would be like. And we had to outline what we would have accomplished by then.

It seems like a silly and fun exercise, but it's so much more than that. It's a masterful way to set intentions and goals.

Some people might create a vision board, which I'm a big fan of, but something about putting pen to paper in your own voice really makes a difference.

When I was working at Fox News, I had a blast for over a decade. I was in the "good old days" Andy Bernard spoke about for most of that time.

I'd already started speaking and had my first book published, but I knew there was more for me. Producing health videos had lost its excitement for me. Coming to work every day became harder and harder.

One day at lunch, I took myself for a walk to a park in Midtown Manhattan, not far from the Sixth Avenue studios.

When I returned to my desk, I wrote this email, which I scheduled (via the plugin Boomerang) to send to myself one year later.

My Letter to Myself

Subject: My thoughts from the park today

I'm writing this on 9/7/16 at 2:44 p.m. I'm sitting at my desk at FOX—*Chopped* is on TV, and I hear sirens outside.

I just returned from that park near 50th street. I went there to get away for a little bit and give myself a break. I sat without a cell phone, with my thoughts (as Oprah says).

I decided that in one year I would be leaving this job. Not to take another job at another media company, but to work for myself. To make double, even triple the amount of money I make now, and to increase my happiness and productivity tenfold.

I'm tired of doing the same thing. And I feel I've established myself enough in this field at this point that it no longer needs to define me. I've written a book on a topic other than my traditional career path, I'm launching an online course called "Lights Camera Expert" with

Terri Trespicio, and I have ideas and things I want to be doing to increase that course and make it thrive.

To stay in this job would hold me back. It's opened doors for me beyond belief, but now I think it's holding some doors closed for me.

This revelation has been a long time coming. Jay [my husband] has been saying it for years. But to admit it to myself is:

1. terrifying
2. overwhelming
3. liberating

Probably in that order.

I'm scheduling this to send to me in one year—because I know from today on I'll take steps to make this idea I had in the park a reality, and I want to keep myself on track!

Fast forward to 9/7/17.

I totally forgot that I had written this email.

I was shocked when I got it because I had just given my notice a few weeks before.

Things had changed on my team. I had a new boss, and things just weren't the same. I'd be leaving to start my own business in October.

It blew my mind.

This email reminded me that I was making the right decision.

Even though I was scared and had my doubts about making the leap into entrepreneurship, it's what I needed to do.

I was pulled back to just how I felt when I was sitting in that park—I was ready for more.

I was in that moment.

I'd love for you to have this opportunity too.

Write a letter to yourself, whether it be here or via email, and set an alarm to read it in one year.

What will you be doing?
Who will you be with?
How will you be feeling?

_____

_____

_____

_____

How Did That Feel?

After you write this letter, document how you feel. Use words to describe what this exercise has done for you:

Schedule It

Take this letter and make sure to send it to yourself in one year. You can either set a reminder in your phone to prompt you to read it (and remind yourself of its location) or schedule an email to youself in the future using an app like BoomerangforGmail.com.

How will you send this letter to yourself in one year?

"There is freedom waiting for you, on the breezes of the sky. And you ask, 'What if I fall?' Oh, but my darling, what if you fly?"

—Erin Hanson

PART THREE

YOUR PASSPORT TO
STRESS-FREE LIVING

As a television producer, my job has been to make sure the right stories get in the right order in a newscast and make it on the air (or on the web) on time. I've used this skill to produce aspects of my life like vacations, my wedding, and even my day-to-day to-dos like finding a new apartment. It's where timing how long activities will take me comes in very handy. That way, I know exactly how long I need to finish a task. If you haven't done this exercise in Part One, I highly recommend it.

Believe it or not, having guidelines will allow you to be freer.

PRODUCE YOUR LIFE

What we'll be doing in this section is fitting the puzzle pieces together so you can design the life you want with as little stress as possible.

You have complete control here. You're the boss, and what you say goes!

There's going to be a fair amount of flipping back and forth through the pages you've already completed, so do what you must to prevent paper cuts.

Think Simple

Simple changes can make a huge difference.

Don't worry if your plan doesn't seem grandiose. It's fine. In fact, it probably shouldn't be over the top because that will be difficult to maintain.

I did a similar activity for my business, and I examined how I wanted to feel at the end of the day. I moved around some things, and it was truly life altering. I'm telling you—just giving myself permission to not take calls on Mondays opened up something for me.

It makes me so happy to get to choose what my days look like.

The fact that I keep my Mondays clear and use them as connection days for lunches, teas, etc. has been tremendous for my psyche and productivity.

Plus, I get to start my week in a fun way that isn't stressful.

"When it is obvious that the goals cannot be reached, don't adjust the goals; adjust the action steps."

—Confucius

LOOK BACK TO LOOK AHEAD

For any of this to work, we need to set up some ground rules for you.

Remember the "Yes vs. No" activity from Part One on page 35? Here's where the flipping back to what you've already filled out comes into play.

That's where you listed out the activities from all aspects of your life that you said YES to in the past year.

Task #1: Flip back there now and identify the top five things from the "Yes List" that fit any of these criteria:

☐ Took up your time
☐ Took up your energy
☐ Stressed you out

1.

2.

3.

4.

5.

Task #2: Flip to Part Two, page 107 where you listed out what you *want* on your "Yes List" going forward.

Pick your top five things from any aspect of your life that you want to be doing more of:

1.

2.

3.

4.

5.

Task #3: Notice anything different? Most likely, those things that you said yes to this year in Part One were not on your list in Part Two. List out here what you'd need to do to make sure the stuff that stressed you out from Part One doesn't end up on your plate again.

_____

_____

_____

_____

_____

_____

_____

_____

What Is Your #1 Priority Right Now?

Flip back to page 33 in Part One and write down here what your biggest priority is right now.

This is the lens which you'll look through for every decision you make going forward.

I know it sounds a bit dramatic, but it doesn't have to be. It's actually freeing to know your priority. If it doesn't align with a task, then you say no to that task as much as you can. As Barefoot Contessa Ina Garten would say, "How easy is that?"

Remind yourself—what is your biggest priority right now?

IT'S YOUR RIGHT TO SAY NO!

We've all done it. You say yes to something everyone wants you to do, well, everyone except the most important person—you! It's difficult to say no, that's for sure. But, once you do, it will change your life.

Your "No Mantra"

Any time you feel tempted to say yes to something that you truly don't want to do, that won't serve you in any way, say these words OUT LOUD:

"I don't have to say yes to everything everyone asks me to do. Life will go on. Period, the end."

Pro Tip: Shoot a quick video of you saying this new mantra and share it with me on social media. Be sure to tag me @ListProducer and use the hashtag #ListfulLiving.

"If your compassion does not include yourself, it is incomplete."

—Jack Kornfield

How to Say No

There are graceful ways to back out of doing something. Here's a few ways:

Be Plain: Tell the person you can't do it and politely decline right away. That way, you don't hold up their plans and they can ask someone else if needed. I find this is the best way to do it. No explanations.

"Thanks for the opportunity, but I won't be able to attend."

PERIOD, THE END. Stop talking! I say this in the most loving way.

This is what I tell all my media-training clients too. People tend to go on and on and on. Just be simple and plain, and then stop talking. It will help your point land more powerfully.

Be Honest: Explain that you have other commitments and just can't make it.

"I'm traveling at that time for a conference and won't be able to make it, but thanks for the invite. Good luck with your event."

Suggest an Alternative: Be of service! Give them a suggestion for another person who could take your place.

"I won't be able to take on this project at this time, but I'd be happy to connect you with Sandra who might be a good fit."

Ask for a Raincheck: Sometimes you don't want to do something right now, but that doesn't mean you may never want to do it. Show good faith and ask to be first in line next time.

"I wish I could make it, but I'll be out of town. Please let me know the dates of the next event so I can block it in my calendar."

Let's Practice Your "No" Speech

Now let's look at Part Two and what you declared that you did not want to do again; let's make sure it doesn't end up on your to-do list.

Task #1: Flip to page 113 and pick the top three things that do NOT get you excited. Write them here:

1.

2.

3.

Task #2: Let's practice what you'll say when someone asks you to do this task again. I know this might seem insane, but trust me on this. I've media-trained lots of authors and experts who think they'll be great once the camera is rolling, and guess what happens? They freeze; they don't know what to say and wish they practiced more. Yep.

So let's do a trial run. Write down the exact quote you'll give in the bubbles below when asked to do those tasks.

Task #3: Say these quotes out loud. It's one thing to write something down, but it's another thing to say it out loud and really feel it. Say each line like you're talking to a person. If you need someone to "talk to," go to my website (ListProducer. com) and practice telling my smiling face no. It's good practice and I won't be offended, I promise.

Task #4: Check in with yourself and see how that felt. Do you think you can do this when faced with a real-life situation?

Write out how you feel about this here:

Task #5: Fill me in on how you felt doing this on social media by using the hashtag #ListfulLiving and tagging me @ ListProducer.

Forget FOMO—Embrace JOMO

You've probably heard of the term FOMO or "fear of missing out"—possibly in the context of someone making fun of millennials who say things like, "I can't believe I'm not going to Coachella this year! I have so much FOMO."

But it's not just millennials who have this problem!

I used to get FOMO, and it drove me a little crazy.

Listen to me: not all opportunities are equal.

I've known this to be more and more true over the past couple of years. It all started when I had my appendix rupture that I told you about. It opened my eyes to that fact that I had been taking on too much, all because of FOMO.

After this, I cut back; I started only taking on projects I knew would be useful and only attending a few key events a year.

The benefits were immediately noticeable. I not only had more time for myself, but I also had the luxury of being able to take more time with my tasks.

I had more concentration and significantly less stress.

Plus, as it turns out, the Internet has coined a new term for this.

JOMO or the Joy of Missing Out.

Its key principles are all about disconnecting from technology, opting out, and having a more minimalist approach to life.

On my blog at ListProducer.com, I shared a story of a sports reporter named Kristin Hewitt who announced that her family would be "doing nothing" for the summer. Or rather that they would be focusing on what they needed most at the time, as opposed to what they felt they should be doing or what looked good on social media. So even if that meant having a "sofa day," they'd do it.

It's not hard to find examples of people taking on the spirit of JOMO and generally checking out in favor of more quality experiences.

Join the JOMO Revolution—Set Rules

So how can you join the JOMO revolution?

Rules are key.

Knowing what you'll agree to and when you'll agree to it is so important.

This not only will make you less stressed out, but it will also give you a sense of control in your life, which can actually be freeing. I know you might be resisting this and thinking it's too rigid. You can bend the rules as needed, but it's important to have guidelines in place so you stay accountable.

Let's work through it together.

WHERE WILL YOU SPEND YOUR TIME?

At Work

I like to have a leisurely morning on workdays. I like to read the newspaper and find out what's going on in the world before I dive into working.

I designed my days so I only take calls (media training, prospective clients, interviews, connection calls, etc.) at 11:30 a.m., 2 p.m., or 3:30 p.m. That's it. Those are my go-to times. I only do those calls on Tuesday, Wednesday, and Thursday if I can help it.

Mondays, as I mentioned, are blocked for connection. I like to book lunches, in-person meetings, and video calls where I'm getting to know people or reconnect.

I blocked Fridays to write this book! And I think I'm going to stick to keeping Fridays for creativity even after the manuscript is turned in. It's been so nice to have a non-negotiable day for my imagination.

The beauty of having regularity and a system like this is that it takes the guesswork out of scheduling.

Too many options lead to indecision and procrastination.

It makes my life less stressful: when someone asks to have lunch, I look at my Monday and if that time is booked I can't do it that week, so we look at the next week. It makes it easier not to overschedule myself this way.

Plus, you better believe when I do get asked to lunch, I have a list of go-to restaurants in hand. This list makes it easy to make plans and go to places that I enjoy.

Over the weekend, I try my hardest not to work too much. When you're an entrepreneur, it's hard to stop working. But I try to be mindful of this!

I do have one call that I've been doing since before my first book, *Listful Thinking*, came out. It's with my editorial assistant Nicole Rouyer Guillet, who helps me maintain my blog and email list for ListProducer.com and PaulaRizzo.com. I certainly would not still be doing blogs every week without her help, so we make it a priority to speak once a week.

Paula's Work Week

Monday	**Connection Day:** Blocked for lunches, in-person meetings, and dinners
Tuesday	**Client Day:** Blocked for media training, strategy consulting, interviews, speaking, etc. Calls at 11:30 a.m., 2 p.m., and 3:30 p.m.
Wednesday	**Client Day:** Blocked for media training, strategy consulting, interviews, speaking, etc. Calls at 11:30 a.m., 2 p.m., and 3:30 p.m.
Thursday	**Client Day:** Blocked for media training, strategy consulting, interviews, speaking, etc. Calls at 11:30 a.m., 2 p.m., and 3:30 p.m.
Friday	**Creativity Day:** Blocked for writing/reading/creating
Saturday	ListProducer.com editorial call
Sunday	FREE!

Fill in Your Ideal Work Week

What will you do on which days and at what time?

Take into account your productivity style that you figured out in Part One. Reference what you wrote on on pages 86 to 90 of Part Two under *Design Your Ideal…*

Monday	
Tuesday	
Wednesday	
Thursday	
Friday	
Saturday	
Sunday	

Fill in Your Ideal Work Month

Are there recurring meetings, events, or conferences that you want to make sure to make time for? Even if you don't have a specific conference name, block off time to explore these ideas. I like to attend one networking event a month if I can.

MONTH – WEEK ONE

1

2

3

4

5

6

7

8

9

10

11

12

13

14

MONTH – WEEK THREE

15

16

17

18

19

20

21

22

23

24

25

26

27

28

29

30

31

At Home

Fill in Your Ideal Home Week

When do you want to cook dinner at home versus go out?
When do you want to entertain friends? Who do you want to
see more often?

Go back to *Design Your Ideal…*in Part Two for inspiration.

Monday	
Tuesday	
Wednesday	
Thursday	
Friday	
Saturday	
Sunday	

Work in Time for Humor

What's so funny about stress?

"We don't want to laugh at things that cause us stress. But, if you can find something within a stressful moment silly or amusing, it actually reduces the stress hormones in the brain, improves the immune system, and helps you to problem solve more effectively."

—Heidi Hanna PhD, co-author, *What's So Funny About Stress? How to Use Healthy Humor to Build Radical Resilience*

Pro Tip: Get a humor buddy!

Find someone you can trade funny texts or humorous photos with. Start training your brain to look for funny things in the world and be more flexible and resilient.

Make a "Just Enough" List

I rave about these all the time, but honestly, they've caused a huge improvement in my productivity.

I learned this idea from my friend and colleague Dr. Heidi Hanna, PhD, who I interviewed in my first book, *Listful Thinking*.

Rather than drowning in task after task, I cherry-pick the few things I absolutely have to do to have a successful day.

As Dr. Hanna instructed, I ask myself, "What would be 'just enough' so that my clients would be happy and I'd meet my deadlines for the day?" It gives me a chance to think about my priorities.

So how about for you? What are three things on your just enough list for today?

1.
2.
3.

Your Ideal Workspace

Go back to Part One on page 46 where you talked about what your workspace looks like now. Then go to Part Two on page 105 where you laid out what your ideal work surroundings would look like. Now bring it to reality. What can you do to make your workspace more inspiring and make you more creative?

Task #1: List out the ways here:

1.
2.
3.
4.
5.

Task #2: Pick one of these ways and set it into motion to start working toward a more inspired workspace.

Your Productivity Power Hours

When do you feel like your most productive self? Before lunch? After lunch?

List out here what times of the day you'll do certain tasks:

MORNING	AFTERNOON	EVENING

RECHARGE YOUR SOUL

Maintaining a to-do list and making sure your calendar is filled with the right things that fit your goals are only part of the puzzle.

You have to factor in some time to recharge your soul, rest, and recuperate.

Here's where your "Checklist of Fun" from Part Two, page 116 comes in.

What helps you to relax and refresh?

Fill in these calendars with what you'd like to do on a weekly and monthly basis to recharge.

WEEK

Monday	
Tuesday	
Wednesday	
Thursday	
Friday	
Saturday	
Sunday	

1

2

3

4

5

6

7

8

9

10

11

12

13

14

15

16

17

18

19

20

21

MONTH – WEEK FOUR

22

23

24

25

26

27

28

29

30

31

Map Out Your Vacation Time

I just love to be in a new place and learning more about it. Part of that fun for me is the research. It's the journalist in me, but I just can't get enough of reading reviews and hearing about other people's experiences.

When I started working for myself as a media trainer and strategist, one of the goals I had was to travel at least once a month.

It could be for a training, a conference, a speaking gig, or vacation and relaxation. But I knew I wanted to do something once a month. For the most part, I've kept to that. And you know why? Because I set the intention for it and made it happen.

You can do the same with whatever it is you'd like to do.

How many vacations would you like to take this year?

How many of those are with family?

How many are on your own?

List out the locations you'd like to visit below and for how long.
Be realistic:

Location	Duration	Travel Companions	Potential Dates

Task #1: Pick one of those trips and write out what needs to happen for you to plan that trip. It could be research, saving money, taking time off, etc. Write it all out in the space below.

Task #2: Pick one thing on this list that you can do this week to get closer to having this trip happen.

Task #3: Put time in your calendar to do this task right now.

Go on a Virtual Vacation

Sometimes you don't even have to leave your home to get the benefits of a vacation.

Take a break from work with a virtual vacation via Google Maps. Pick a spot and use the street view to zoom around and get inspired. Or I really love the app TripScout, which was created by my friend Konrad Waliszewski. It curates the best articles and videos for destinations around the world. I love to open it in the morning, get inspired, and daydream about my next trip.

Social Hour

Who are the people in your life you'd like to spend time with who will make you feel calm and less stressed?

Look back at Part Two at your "Priority People" list on page 101. It's time to put those people on your calendar.

Priority Person	How often will you see them?	What will you do?	Potential dates

Task #1: Pick one of these priority people and write out what needs to happen for you to plan out your time together. It can be a phone call, a trip together, a lunch, etc. Write it all out in the space below.

Priority Person: _____

What needs to happen to plan a get-together?

Task #2: Pick one thing on this list that you can do this week to plan to see this priority person.

Task #3: Put time in your calendar to do this task right now.

REPEAT

Now that you have these guidelines, go ahead and do this for everyone else on your list and put them on your calendar. This will be a continuous plan that you can use again and again.

Produce Your Self-Care Calendar

This is all about you! This is your time.

Go back to Part Two where you worked on the "Renew with Self-Care" section. You'll need it for this exercise, but maybe some other ideas popped into your head since filling that in; that's perfectly fine.

This is a work in progress and will change over time. What makes you feel renewed might be different at different times in your life.

The most important thing to remember is to schedule time for yourself.

It's easier said than done, because it requires some discipline. When you see a self-care activity on your calendar, it's key to treat it like you would any other appointment and respect it.

You are just as important as everyone else. Don't forget that.

Task #1: List out the top five small activities that will make you feel happy and recharged. These can be things like naps, a phone call with a friend, taking a walk, etc.

1.
2.
3.

4.

5.

Task #2: Ok, now how do we integrate these things into your life as it is right now? Let's define when you'll do these fabulous things. Write here, along with how often you'd like to do them:

Self-care activity	How often will you do this?	Who will be with you?	Potential dates

Task #3: Put them on your actual calendar.

Whether you use a smartphone or a paper calendar, take the time right now to do this.

My best friend, Nicole Feldman, won't part with her pocket-sized paper calendar, which she calls "Granny." It cracks me up every time she refers to it that way, but it works for her! I prefer to put everything in my smartphone, but she's more old school about her calendar. Try both ways and see which you like better.

Put ten minutes on the clock and go!

Don't worry about starting these activities right away—you can schedule just a few things every month and build from there. If you do just one self-care activity this month, that's way better than last month, right?

Task #4: Stick to it! Every time you see one of these activities in your calendar, you must do it. That's the point! You have to stick to this plan to make it work.

Do not reschedule with yourself—give yourself time to recharge.

DESIGN A SUPPORT TEAM

Setting yourself up for success is so important if you want to truly make a change.

To do that, you need to look at the people around you and see who will support your efforts and who will not. And then fill in the blanks and add people to your team at home and at work.

Let's ramp up your support team.

Who can you count on to help you when you need some time for productivity or to recharge? List them out here:

Support person	What can they help with?	How often?

For me, my husband, friends, and family help tremendously when I need support personally, but I also use support in my business. I wouldn't be able to do what I do and be productive without these helping hands.

Virtual Assistant

I looked at where I was spending my time and decided I needed extra help, so I hired an amazing virtual assistant through Peachtree VA. I realized that if I wanted to grow my business, write this book, speak at conferences, travel with my husband and friends, and find time for my own self-care—I couldn't do it without help. Tabitha Bethelmy, my assistant, helps me with so many tasks including:

- Scheduling appointments

- Sending my media-training clients homework and resources

- Coordinating my own media interviews

- Keeping track of business development opportunities

- Putting the right things on my to-do list

- Sending gifts

- Doing research

- Making travel arrangements

- And so much more

I knew I needed some help with administrative tasks when I booked a flight for the wrong week and had to pay a two hundred dollars change fee! I'm very capable of making travel arrangements myself; however, I was stretched too thin and needed help. Maybe there's an incident like that in your own life that is a whisper that you're doing too much yourself.

List off some of the tasks that you do on a regular basis that are not the best use of your skills and expertise:

_____

_____

_____

_____

_____

_____

_____

_____

_____

_____

Just because you CAN do it yourself doesn't mean you SHOULD!

Writing Partner

People often ask how I'm able to churn out so much content. The answer is not on my own. I learned this as a television producer, because it took a team to produce quality content consistently.

My intern-turned-editorial-assistant Nicole Rouyer Guillet is truly the reason why ListProducer.com's blog still exists.

She helps me come up with ideas, write posts, and schedule them to be published as well as getting any social media messages out.

If you ever catch a "Britishism" in one of my posts, it's probably Nicole—I've tried to break her of the habit (since she's in England and I'm in America) but sometimes they still slip in! I'm so grateful for her partnership and enthusiasm for lists.

Same goes for writing content like this book. I needed accountability and a writing partner to keep me productive. Sarah Montana was my writing partner for this book, and I'm so thankful to her. She's working on her own memoir and is also a screenwriter for the Hallmark Channel. We'd meet at a coffee shop in New York City, talk for a bit, and then get rolling along on writing. We'd time ourselves and check in every once in a while.

You may not be a writer, but you may have a project that you need to get done and could use an accountability buddy to help with. List off those projects here and who might help you:

Project	Accountability partner?

Bookkeeper

I have a bookkeeper who I adore named Shel Mitchell of Down to Earth Accounting. He keeps me Zen about money. We meet every single month to go over the numbers, and he keeps me on track for my goals and tells me when I need to hit the gas and find more clients. Working with him has been a great way for me to remain calm in my business. Knowledge really is power and having someone by your side is key.

Mastermind

As a journalist, it's part of my training to find the best expert to explain something I don't understand. When I first went into business for myself, I wanted to know from the experts how to do it right. I joined a mastermind group run by Lisa Sasevich to learn how to do sales and more speaking engagements. I joined a peer mastermind group with Terri Trespicio, Jenny Powers, and Farnoosh Torabi who are three successful entrepreneurs and friends in New York City. We speak about business and help each other out whenever possible. I wanted to have pillars of support in my life who I could turn to whenever I needed.

TOOLS TO MAKE LIFE EASIER

These are just a few of the tools that I use to make my life easier and be more productive and less stressed. For more, check out my blog at ListProducer.com.

Calm: I talked about meditation and the benefits at the beginning of this book. But the most important thing with this and everything else you decide to implement is to make sure it works for you. I use the Calm app to meditate for ten minutes a day. I find that just enough, and I stick to it every morning. Calm.com

Timeshifter: I love this app when I travel because it helps to eliminate jet lag. Jet Lag is one of the worst productivity killers. When I'm speaking at a conference or event, it's so important to be on my game. This app tells you when you should sleep, eat, see sunlight, and avoid caffeine as you travel across time zones. Timeshifter.com

Asana: Want to make sure you can keep track of your to-do list digitally and collaborate with your team? I love Asana for this. I use it with my assistant all the time, and we can keep track of ongoing projects and eliminate unnecessary emails. Asana.com

The Skimm: The news junkie in me loves to know what's going on in the world, but I don't want to be bogged down with too much to read. Just give me the highlights please! It's much more productive to read TheSkimm.com every morning, because it gives you bite-sized news that is, well, skimmable.

Marco Polo: This is a great app that allows you to send video messages to people via your phone. I make all my media-training clients download this app to become more comfortable on camera. But it's also an amazing productivity tool. You can keep in contact with friends and family more easily. MarcoPolo.me

BombBomb: I was so excited when I found this resource. It's a way to be face to face with people in your inbox. You can speak to potential clients, past clients, anyone with an email address really, and send them video messages instead of typing. This saves time when you're too busy for a phone call; plus, sometimes an email doesn't really explain what you mean. So you could just leave a video message for someone and keep the ball rolling on your project. BombBomb.com

KEEP THE MOMENTUM GOING

This is where the rubber meets the road. It's time to get serious about not only implementing these strategies that you've laid out for yourself but also keeping the momentum going.

Here are a few ways to do it. Check off which ones will work for you:

- ☐ Accountability buddy
- ☐ An assistant
- ☐ Build out your calendar for the year
- ☐ Set a goal
- ☐ Give yourself a reward
- ☐ Say it out loud
- ☐ Tell someone what your goals are
- ☐ Put goals on your to-do list
- ☐ _____
- ☐ _____
- ☐ _____
- ☐ _____
- ☐ _____
- ☐ _____

Once you've picked the ways you're going to keep this going, let me know! Post it on social media using the hashtag #ListfulLiving and tag me @ListProducer.

CELEBRATE!

Let's take a moment to look back at what you've done, because it's a big deal. I'm all about pausing to celebrate the little wins in life and getting through this book is a win!

YAY!

Write down a prize you'll give yourself for finishing this book. It could be reading a chapter from a novel, watching a show on Netflix, calling a friend, etc. Write it down here and put it in your calendar so you can claim your reward!

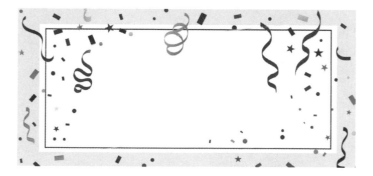

Good for you. You're obviously committed to stress-free living. This final part is critical to set the wheels in motion.

Keep in Touch

I'd love to hear from you! Please drop me an email at Paula@ listproducer.com if you have any questions or want to share your aha's! Or even better share with me on social media where my handle is @ListProducer. Use #ListfulLiving too.

If you enjoyed this book, please consider posting a review on Amazon. Even if it's only a few words, it would be a huge help. Bit.ly/ListfulLiving

Listful Living Hub

I put together a toolkit just for you at ListProducer.com/ ListfulLivingHub.

There, you'll find videos and tips from me to you. I'll dive in even deeper on ways to use this journal to reach your goals and be less stressed.

THANK YOU LIST

Thank you to everyone who supported me and my list-making ways through the years! I'm grateful for each and every one of you including:

Julia Andrews
Tabitha Bethelmy
Irene Berman
Jay Berman
Robert Berman
Joya Dass
Laura DeAngelis
Nicole Feldman
Peter Feldman
Heidi Hanna
Sharon Hazelrigg
Suzanne Kingsbury
Brenda Knight
Cass McCrory
Ben Michaelis
Sarah Montana
Jenny Powers
Carolyn Reilly

Michele Reilly
Olga Rizzo
Louis Rizzo
Rita Rosenkranz
Nicole Rouyer Guillet
Sandra Schustack
Peter Shankman
Farnoosh Torabi
Terri Trespicio
Jennifer Walsh
Women's Media Group
The ListProducer.com
blog readers
Listful Living VIP
Launch Team

ABOUT THE AUTHOR

Paula Rizzo is an Emmy-award winning television producer, bestselling author, and media trainer and strategist. She's the founder of ListProducer.com and the author of *Listful Thinking: Using Lists to Be More Productive, Highly Successful and Less Stressed*.

Paula's work has been featured on TV, print, radio, and around the web. She's a frequent speaker and has presented at the MA Conference for Women, HOW Design Live, New York Women in Communications, Public Relations Society of America (PRSA), National Association of Professional Organizers (NAPO), American Society of Association Executives, and many others. She lives in Manhattan with her husband, Jay Berman. Go to PaulaRizzo.com for more.

Mango Publishing, established in 2014, publishes an eclectic list of books by diverse authors—both new and established voices—on topics ranging from business, personal growth, women's empowerment, LGBTQ studies, health, and spirituality to history, popular culture, time management, decluttering, lifestyle, mental wellness, aging, and sustainable living. We were recently named 2019's #1 fastest growing independent publisher by *Publishers Weekly*. Our success is driven by our main goal, which is to publish high quality books that will entertain readers as well as make a positive difference in their lives.

Our readers are our most important resource; we value your input, suggestions, and ideas. We'd love to hear from you—after all, we are publishing books for you!

Please stay in touch with us and follow us at:

Facebook: Mango Publishing
Twitter: @MangoPublishing
Instagram: @MangoPublishing
LinkedIn: Mango Publishing
Pinterest: Mango Publishing

Sign up for our newsletter at www.mango.bz and receive a free book!

Join us on Mango's journey to reinvent publishing, one book at a time.